STARK LIBRARY

T4-ADP-478

INCREDIBLE CHANGES ON EARTH

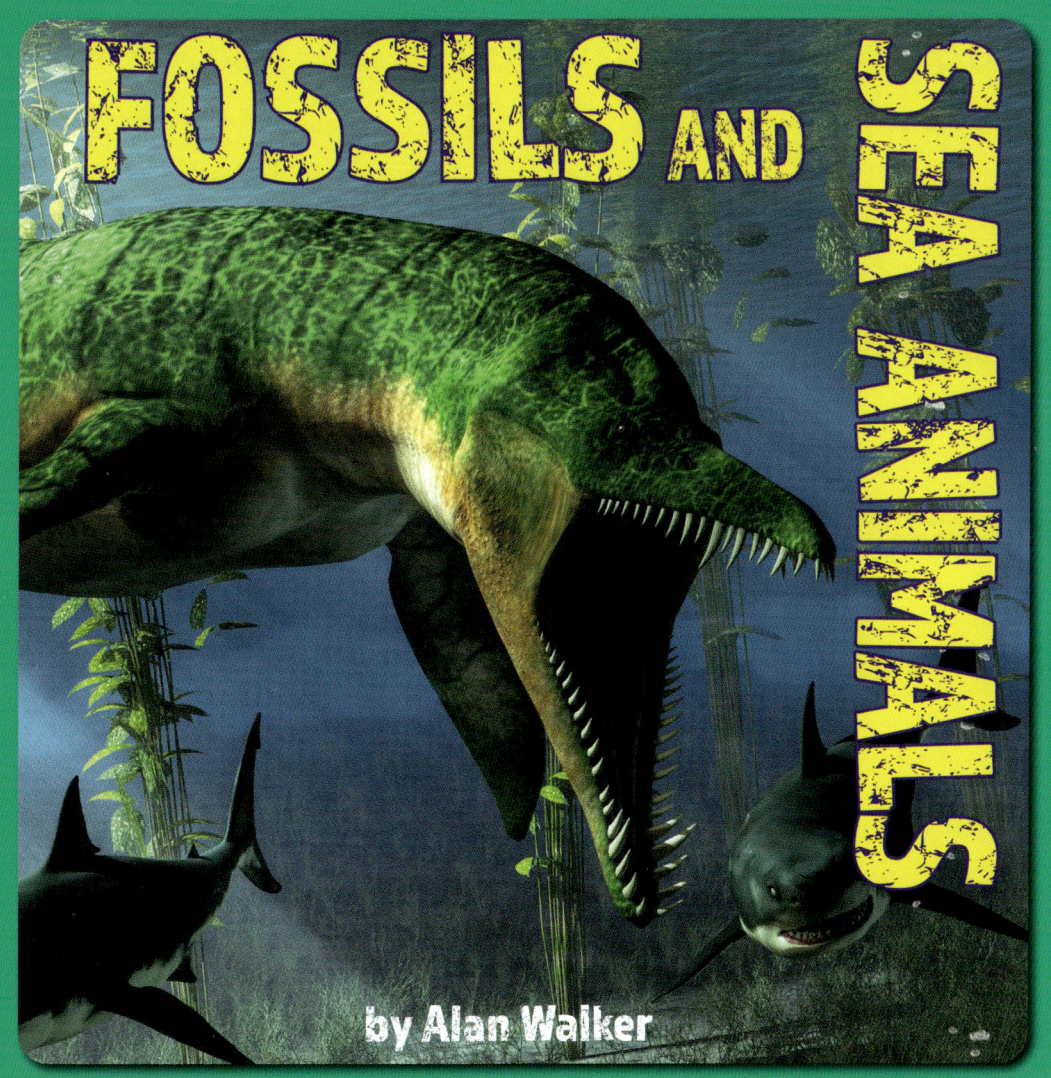

FOSSILS AND SEA ANIMALS

by Alan Walker

A Crabtree Seedlings Book

CRABTREE
Publishing Company
www.crabtreebooks.com

Paleontology (pay-lee-uhn-TOL-uh-jee):
the study of ancient life using fossils

Elasmosaurus
(eh-lazz-muh-SOR-uhss)
Lived: 85 million to 65 million years ago

Elasmosaurus lived in water, but breathed air. It grew to more than 40 feet (12 meters) long.

TABLE OF CONTENTS

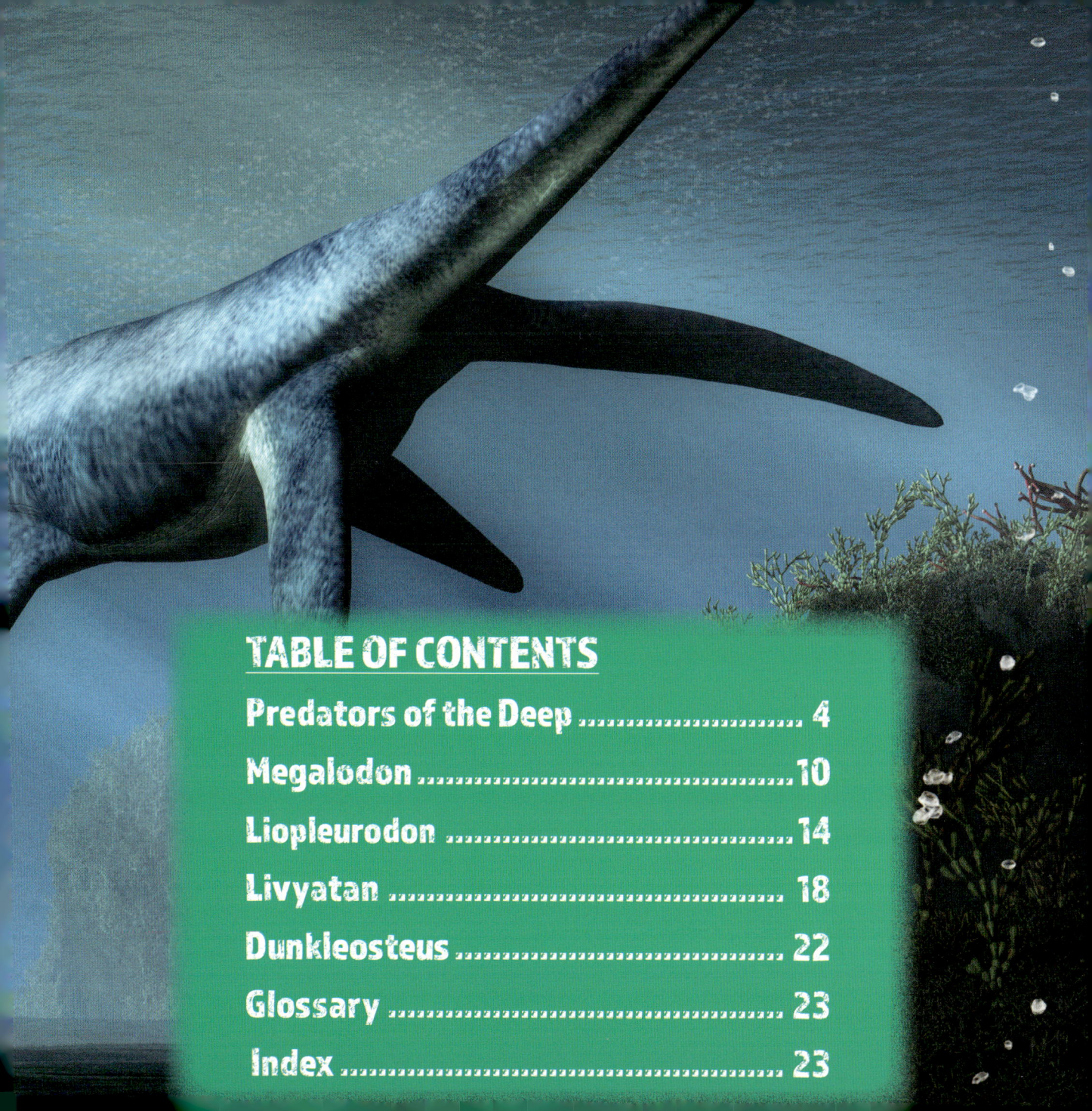

Predators of the Deep 4
Megalodon 10
Liopleurodon 14
Livyatan 18
Dunkleosteus 22
Glossary 23
Index 23

Predators of the Deep

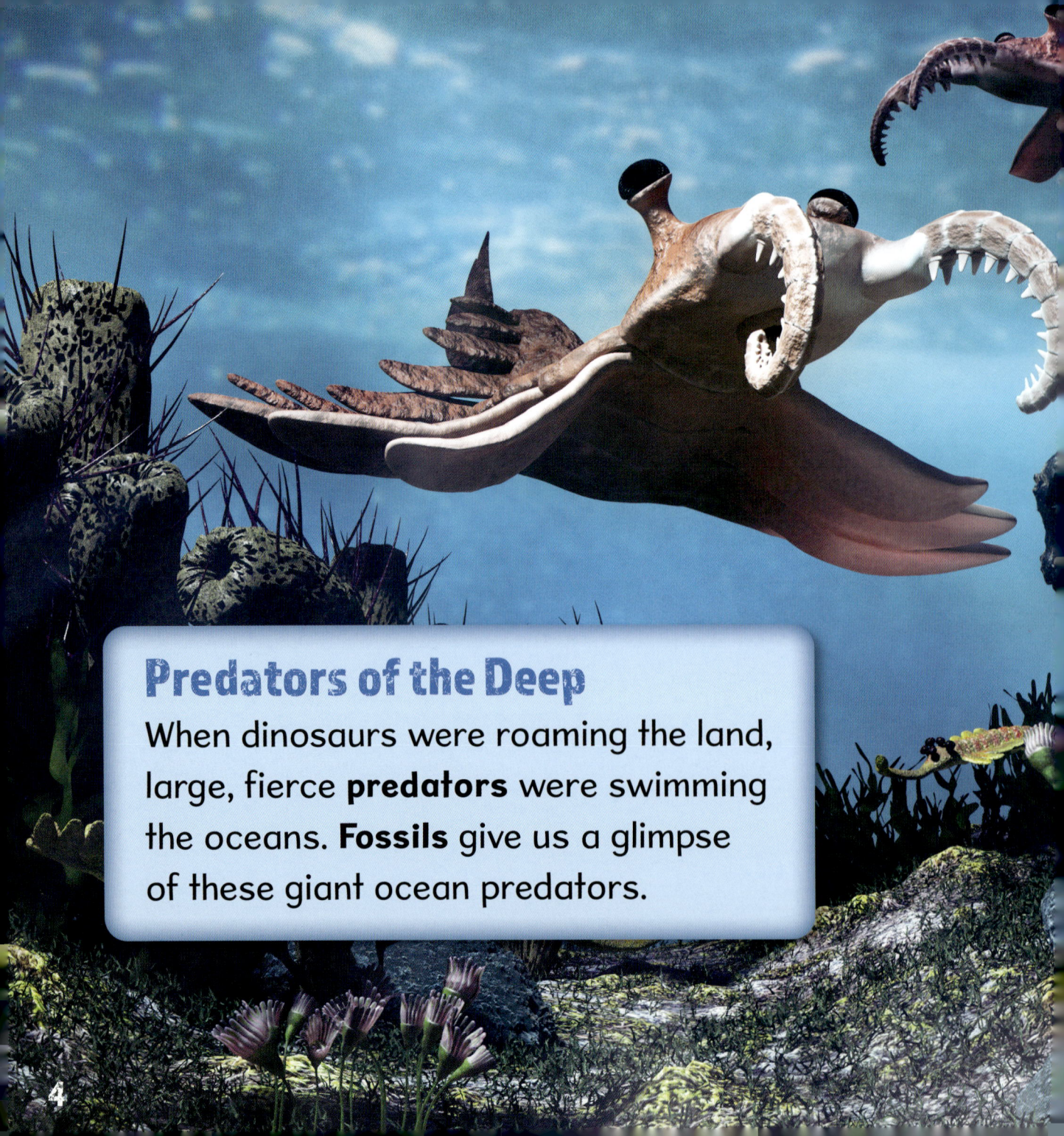

When dinosaurs were roaming the land, large, fierce **predators** were swimming the oceans. **Fossils** give us a glimpse of these giant ocean predators.

Skeleton of an *Elasmosaurus*

5

6

Like the dinosaurs, most of these large and fierce ocean predators are now **extinct**. But we can still learn a lot about them through fossils.

Fossils can tell us if the animal lived on land or in water. They can also tell us what it ate, how it moved, when it died, and many other things.

8

Scientists can compare fossils to living animals today. Clues from fossils show which animals today are living **relatives** of these giant ocean predators.

Megalodon

Thought to be a relative of today's great white shark, the megalodon was a beast.

By studying megalodon teeth, scientists have worked out that megalodons grew to more than 50 feet (15 meters) long.

A jawbone from a megalodon shows how huge these sea animals were!

Megalodon
(mehg-a-LO-don)

Lived: 20 million to 3.6 million years ago

The megalodon holds the record as the largest shark to ever live in our oceans.

How a 6-foot (1.8-meter) modern diver might compare to the ancient megalodon.

The megalodon is thought to have eaten large animals, such as whales. It used its teeth and jaws to crush its **prey**.

Fossil of a megalodon tooth

13

Liopleurodon

Liopleurodon was a large **reptile**. It had lungs and had to surface to breathe air.

Known as a fast swimmer, some scientists think it grew to nearly 26 feet (8 meters) long.

Liopleurodon
(LEE-oh-PLOOR-oh-don)
Lived: 160 million to 155 million years ago

Liopleurodon likely ate whales and seals.

A fossil of a *Liopleurodon* skull

Liopleurodon is part of a group of animals called plesiosaurs. They had **elongated** heads and long flippers.

17

Livyatan

Livyatan is an extinct sperm whale. It was a massive 50 feet (15 meters) in length and had teeth that were 12 inches (30 centimeters) long.

A fossil of a *Livyatan* skull

19

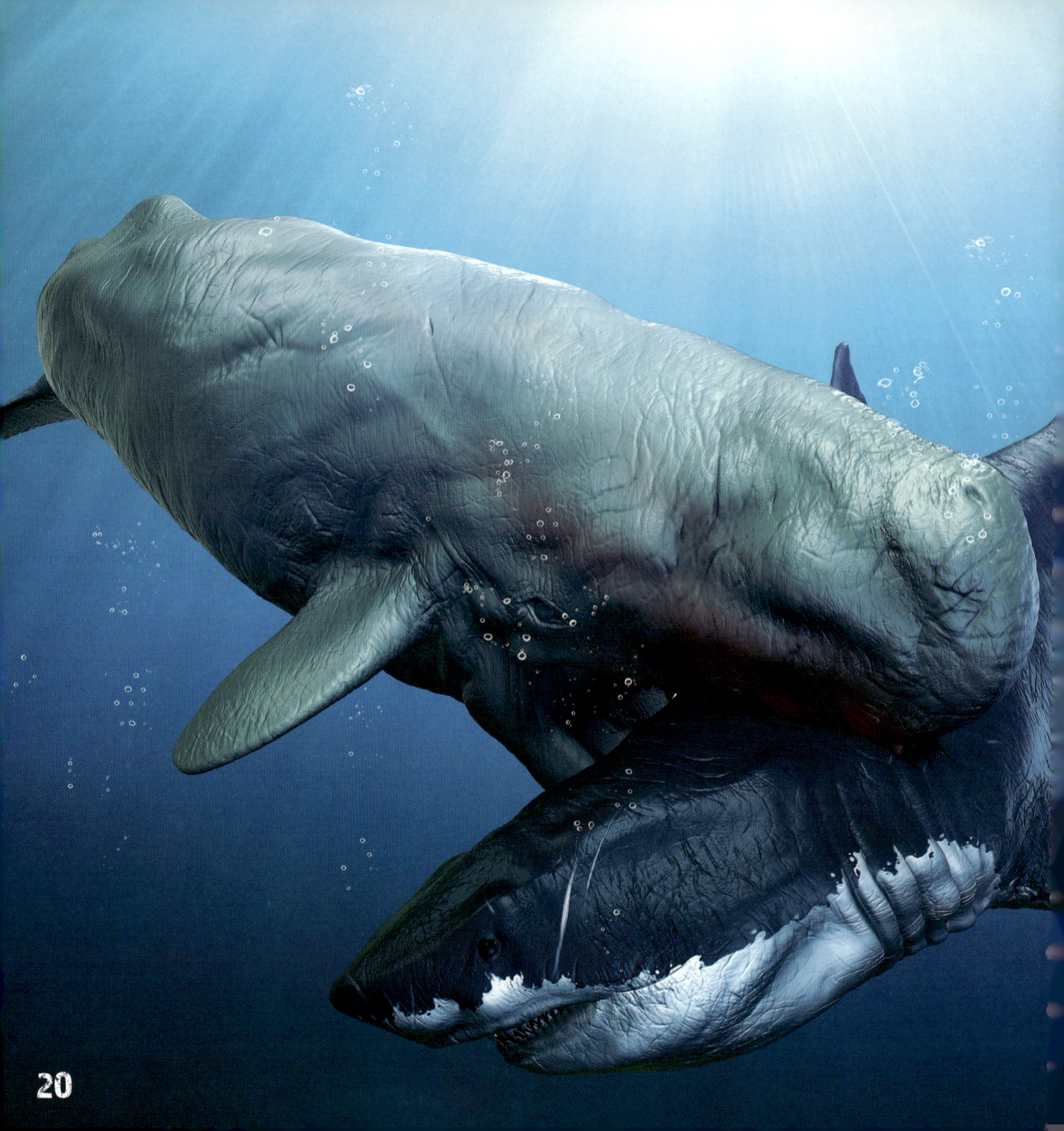

Livyatan is thought to have been an **apex predator.** It competed with megalodon for food. It would have been an amazing battle between these two large animals.

Livyatan
(li-vee-AH-tahn)
Lived: 13 million to 12 million years ago

Livyatan most likely ate smaller whales and sharks.

Dunkleosteus

Dunkleosteus was a powerful predator. Its skull was covered in thick, bony plates. Some of the plates were shaped like fangs and used as teeth.

Dunkleosteus
(dunk-lee-OSS-tee-uhs)

Lived: 370 million to 360 million years ago

Dunkleosteus was almost 20 feet (6 meters) long. It was so powerful that only another *Dunkleosteus* would have been able to kill it.

Glossary

apex predator (AY-peks PRED-uh-tur): An animal that hunts other animals for food and is at the top, or the apex, of the food chain

elongated (ee-LONG-gate-id): Long and thin, stretched out

extinct (ek-STINGKT): No longer alive or existing

fossils (FOSS-uhlz): The remains of animals and plants from long ago, preserved in rock

predators (PRED-uh-turz): Animals that hunt other animals for food

prey (PRAY): Animals that are hunted and eaten by other animals

relatives (REL-uh-tivz): Members of a family

reptile (REP-tile): A cold-blooded animal that has a backbone and lays eggs

Index

Dunkleosteus 22
fossil(s) 4, 7, 9, 13, 15, 18
Liopleurodon 14, 15, 16
Livyatan 18, 21

megalodon 10, 11, 12, 13, 21
predator(s) 4, 7, 9, 21
reptile 14
teeth 10, 12, 18, 22

School-to-Home Support for Caregivers and Teachers

This book helps children grow by letting them practice reading. Here are a few guiding questions to help the reader build his or her comprehension skills. Possible answers appear here in red.

Before Reading
- **What do I think this book is about?** I think this book is about giant sea animals that lived millions of years ago. I think this book is about how scientists use fossils to learn about sea animals.
- **What do I want to learn about this topic?** I want to learn more about different kinds of ancient sea animals. I want to learn about the life expectancy of ancient giant sea animals.

During Reading
- **I wonder why...** I wonder why ancient sea animals became extinct. I wonder why scientists compare fossils to living animals today.

- **What have I learned so far?** I have learned that megalodons are believed to have grown to more than 50 feet (15 meters) long. I have learned that scientists believe that today's great white sharks are related to the megalodon.

After Reading
- **What details did I learn about this topic?** I have learned that extinct means no longer alive or existing. I have learned that an apex predator is an animal that hunts other animals for food and is at the top of the food chain.
- **Read the book again and look for the glossary words.** I see the word *predators* on page 4, and the word *reptile* on page 14. The other glossary words are found on page 23.

Library and Archives Canada Cataloguing in Publication

CIP available at Library and Archives Canada

Library of Congress Cataloging-in-Publication Data

CIP available at Library of Congress

Crabtree Publishing Company
www.crabtreebooks.com   1–800–387–7650

Written by: Alan Walker
Production coordinator and Prepress technician: Tammy McGarr
Print coordinator: Katherine Berti

Print book version produced jointly with Blue Door Education in 2022

Printed in the U.S.A./CG20210915/012022

Content produced and published by Blue Door Education, Melbourne Beach FL USA. This title Copyright Blue Door Education. All rights reserved. No part of this book may be reproduced or utilized in any form or by any means, electronic or mechanical including photocopying, recording, or by any information storage and retrieval system without permission in writing from the publisher.

PHOTO CREDITS:
istock.com, shutterstock.com, Cover and title page: istock.com/Daniel Eskridge, PGs 2-3: istock.com/Daniel Eskridge, PGs 4-5: shutterstock.com/Dotted Yeti - shutterstock.com/Karen Culp, PGs 6-7: shutterstock.com/Joaquin Corbalan P, PGs 8-9: istock.com/Trassnick - shutterstock.com/stockphoto-graf, PGs 10-11 and back cover: shutterstock.com/warpaint - shutterstock.com/Igor Kovalchu - istock.com/GlobalStock, PGs 12-13: shutterstock.com/Nico Ott - shutterstock.com/Elenarts - istock.com/OSTILL, PGs 14-15: istock.com/MR1805 - shutterstock.com/Jaroslav Moravcik, PGs 16-17: istock.com/Daniel Eskridge - istock.com/OSTIL, PGs 18-19: istock.com/OSTIL, shutterstock.com/Herschel Hoffmeyer - Ghedoghedo, CCA-Share Alike4.0 International, PGs 20-21: shutterstock.com/Herschel Hoffmeyer, PGs 22: shutterstock.com/warpaint

Published in the United States
Crabtree Publishing
347 Fifth Ave.
Suite 1402-145
New York, NY 10016

Published in Canada
Crabtree Publishing
616 Welland Ave.
St. Catharines, Ontario
L2M 5V6

3 1333 05203 9250